SALLY'S PHONE

Do you have a phone? Who do you call? Who calls *you*? Can you live without your phone?

Sally has a phone, and a busy life. She gets many phone calls – mostly from her boyfriend, Andrew. Andrew likes telling Sally what to do – and what to wear.

Sally and Andrew are going to a party tonight. 'Wear your blue skirt', says Andrew. But Sally can't wear it – it's dirty, so she has to go shopping for a new one.

But when Sally goes shopping she gets more than just a new skirt – she gets something that will change her life.

OXFORD BOOKWORMS LIBRARY
Human Interest

Sally's Phone

Starter (250 headwords)

CHRISTINE LINDOP

Sally's Phone

Illustrated by
Gavin Reece

OXFORD UNIVERSITY PRESS

OXFORD

UNIVERSITY PRESS

Great Clarendon Street, Oxford OX2 6DP

Oxford University Press is a department of the University of Oxford.
It furthers the University's objective of excellence in research, scholarship,
and education by publishing worldwide in

Oxford New York

Auckland Cape Town Dar es Salaam Hong Kong Karachi
Kuala Lumpur Madrid Melbourne Mexico City Nairobi
New Delhi Shanghai Taipei Toronto

With offices in

Argentina Austria Brazil Chile Czech Republic France Greece
Guatemala Hungary Italy Japan Poland Portugal Singapore
South Korea Switzerland Thailand Turkey Ukraine Vietnam

OXFORD and OXFORD ENGLISH are registered trade marks of
Oxford University Press in the UK and in certain other countries

ISBN: 978 0 19 423426 9

A complete recording of this Bookworms edition of
Sally's Phone is available on audio CD. ISBN 978 0 19 423408 5

Printed in China

Word count (main text): 1400

For more information on the Oxford Bookworms Library, visit
www.oup.com/bookworms

This book is printed on paper from certified and well-managed sources.

CONTENTS

1 Morning

It is Thursday morning. Sally is in bed. Suddenly – Ring ring! Her phone is ringing – but where is it?

Sally gets out of bed and looks in her bag. No phone. She looks under the bed. No phone. Then she looks behind the door. There is her phone. Sally picks up her phone and answers it.

'Hello Sally, it's Andrew.'

Andrew is Sally's boyfriend. He has got a lot of money and a beautiful and expensive car.

'Andrew, it's only seven o'clock—'

'Don't forget, Sally – we're meeting Michael tonight. It's an important evening, because Michael's my new boss. Wear your blue skirt, Sally, I like that skirt. I must go now. See you at half past six. Bye.'

'But Andrew . . . Bye.'

'I can't wear the blue skirt,' Sally thinks. 'It's dirty. What can I wear?'

Sally is having breakfast with her mother and her brother Jack.

'I'm going out tonight,' Sally tells her mother. 'Andrew and I are meeting his new boss.'

'Andrew?' Jack says. 'Huh!'

'Oh be quiet, Jack,' Sally says. 'Andrew is very nice to me.'

'Nice?' Jack says. 'Huh! "Sally, I want a sandwich." "Yes, Andrew." "Sally, I don't like your hair." "No, Andrew, sorry Andrew." "Sally—"'

But then Sally stands up, and Jack runs out of the room.

Sally gets on the train. There are a lot of people on the train. Most of them are talking on their phones.

'John? John! Get up and go to work. It's late!'

'Have you got my money? I need it today. I must have it today.'

'Remember – go to the supermarket tonight. Don't forget!'

And Sally is listening to Andrew.

'Sally, meet me at six o'clock, not at half past six. OK?'

'OK Andrew – but my blue skirt—'

'I must go, Sally – bye.'

Then the train goes into a tunnel. The people on the train can not talk on their phones. They must talk to the other people on the train.

'Hello, Max! How are you?'

'Oh, hello Graham! I'm very well.'

'Where are you working now, Lucy?'

'I'm in a new office in Bank Street.'

'Those are nice shoes, Jane.'

'Thank you, Mary.'

After three minutes, the train comes out of the tunnel. Everyone talks on their phones again.

'Hello? John? Are you out of bed now?'

Now Sally is at work. She is talking to her friend Claire, and she tells her about Andrew, Michael, and the blue skirt.

'It's OK, Sally,' Claire says. 'Let's go out at lunchtime. We can find a new skirt. You can wear it tonight.'

Later, Claire and Sally are having coffee with Louise. She works with them.

Ring ring! It is Andrew again.

'Hi, Sally. Look, meet me at the Bar Bogart, not the Cosmo Bar – OK? The Bar Bogart is nearer. Bye.'

'Bar Bogart,' Claire says. 'Mmm – that's nice.'

'Huh!' Louise says. 'Forget him, Sally. Who needs men? "Do this, do that, go there, don't go there." Huh!'

2 Lunchtime

It is one o'clock. Sally and Claire are looking at skirts.

'Do you like this one, Sally?' Claire says.

'Yes, it's beautiful, but I never wear red.'

'Do you like red?' Claire asks.

'Yes, I do – but Andrew doesn't.'

'Well,' Claire says, 'it's a beautiful skirt. You like red. What do you want to do?'

Sally buys the skirt.

Claire goes back to work, but Sally wants a coffee. She goes into a café. She buys a coffee and sits down. Then she phones her mother.

'Hi, Mum. I've got a new skirt – it's beautiful! I want to wear it tonight.'

'What colour is it?'

'It's red.'

'That's nice. Red is a good colour for you,' says her mother.

Next to Sally, Paul is finishing his coffee. He phones his friend and talks to him. Then he stands up. The bag with the red skirt falls on the floor.

'Oh! I'm sorry,' Paul says. He puts down his phone and picks up the bag. 'Here's your bag.'

'That's OK,' Sally says. 'Thank you.' She smiles.

'What a nice smile!' Paul thinks.

Paul picks up his phone and goes out of the café. Sally finishes her coffee. She picks up her bag and her phone, and goes back to work.

Paul is in his office.

Ring ring!

'What's that noise?' Paul thinks. He answers the phone. It is Andrew.

'Hello, Sally?'

'It's not Sally, it's Paul.'

'Paul? Paul who? Where's Sally?'

'Who's Sally? There's no Sally here.'

'Huh!'

Andrew finishes the call.

Paul wants to phone his mother. He finds 'Mum' on the phone, and presses the button.

'Hello, Mum. It's Paul.'

'Paul? Who's Paul? I'm not Paul's Mum. I'm Sally's Mum and Jack's Mum.'

'What's happening?' Paul thinks.

'What number is that?' he asks.

'It's 0783 491839.'

'I'm very sorry,' Paul says. 'It's the wrong number.'

'That's OK,' Sally's Mum says. 'What a nice voice!' she thinks.

11

Sally is at work.

Ring ring!

'What's that noise?' Sally thinks. She answers the phone.

'Hello, is Paul there?'

'No, I'm sorry, this—'

'Can you give a message to him? This is his sister Katharine. There's a party at my house tonight. It's my birthday.'

'But I—'

'8 o'clock – OK? Bye.'

Sally talks to Claire and Louise.

'I've got a message for Paul – but who's Paul? Do you know a Paul, Claire?' she asks.

'No. What's the message?' Claire asks.

'It's his sister Katharine's birthday, and she's having a party tonight. Do you think it's a wrong number?'

'Yes, I think it is,' Claire says.

'Hey, Sally!' Louise says. 'Put on your red skirt and go to the party. Forget Andrew!'

Paul talks to a friend at work.

'This is Sally's phone – and Sally's got my phone.'

'But who is Sally?'

'I don't know,' says Paul.

'Why don't you phone her?'

'What's my number?' Paul asks. 'I don't know my number.'

'Why not?'

'Because I never call my number!'

Paul phones his mother.

'Mum, what's the number of my phone?'

'Why do you want your phone number, Paul?'

'Because Sally's got my phone.'

'Who's Sally?' his mother asks.

'I don't know, but she's got my phone, and I've got her phone.'

'I don't understand.'

'I know,' says Paul. 'It doesn't matter. Have you got my number?'

'Here it is. 0781 644834.'

'Thanks, Mum.'

Paul phones Sally.

'Hello, Sally – this is Paul.'

'Paul – are you Katharine's brother?' Sally asks.

'Yes, that's right. And I've got your phone.'

'My phone? Oh – wait a minute. The Café Cuba at lunchtime? The bag on the floor?'

'Yes, that's right. Well, we need to change phones.'

'OK – where are you now, Paul?'

'In College Road. I work there.'

'I work in Manchester Street. Can we meet in Queen's Square?' Sally asks.

'OK. What time do you finish work?'

'At half past five.'

'Let's meet in Queen's Square at a quarter to six,' says Paul. 'Phone me then.'

'OK, Paul,' says Sally.

4 Evening

It is half past five. Sally puts on her new skirt.

'Do you like it, Louise?' she asks.

'Oh yes. It's very nice.'

It is twenty to six. Paul arrives in Queen's Square. He looks for Sally. Is that Sally? He can not remember. He phones Sally.

'Hello, Sally. It's Paul. I'm in Queen's Square.'

'Hello, Paul. I'm coming.'

There are lots of people in Queen's Square, and many of them are talking on phones.

Which is Paul? Sally can not remember. She phones Paul.

'Paul – have you got black hair?'

'No, I haven't.'

'Good!' Sally thinks.

'Have you got a book in your hand?' asks Sally.

'No, I haven't.'

'Good!' Sally thinks.

Sally can not find Paul.

'Where are you, Paul?'

'I'm near the trees.'

Sally goes across the square to the trees.

'Are you Paul?' Sally says.

Paul looks at Sally. 'She's beautiful!' he thinks.

'Yes, I'm Paul.'

'He's nice!' Sally thinks.

'I'm Sally. So – we meet again.'

'I'm sorry about your phone, Sally. Here it is.'
'That's OK. Here's your phone, Paul.'
'Sally – would you like a drink? I want to say sorry.'
'OK, but I haven't got much time.'
Paul looks for a bar.
'Let's go to the Blue Moon. We can have a drink there.'

Paul and Sally are at the Blue Moon. Sally sits down at a table. Paul brings their drinks.

'Here's your drink, Sally. And I am sorry about your phone.'

'Forget it, Paul – it doesn't matter. Oh, I've got a message for you. It's from your sister Katharine.'

'From Katharine? What is it?'

'She says that it's her birthday today, and there's a party at her house.'

'Oh no!' Paul says. 'I always forget birthdays. What can I do?'

Sally looks across the square. Near the trees a woman is selling flowers.

'Buy some flowers for your sister, and take them to the party,' she says to Paul.

'Of course! That's the answer. Look, Sally – do you want to come to the party with me? Katharine always has good parties.'

'Well, I . . .' Sally says.

'Oh, I must tell you,' Paul says. 'I've got a message for you from Andrew. He says—'

'It doesn't matter, Paul,' says Sally. 'I don't want the message. I would like to go to the party with you. But I must do something before we go.'

Sally takes her phone out of her bag and turns it off.

In the Bar Bogart, Andrew phones Sally. Sally does not answer. 'Sally?' says Andrew. 'Sally? Answer me!'

Sally and Paul leave the Blue Moon.

'That's a nice skirt,' says Paul. 'I like red.'

Sally smiles at him.

GLOSSARY

bar a place where people can buy and have drinks

birthday the day when your age changes

boss the person that you work for

boyfriend a man or boy that a girl likes and goes out with

button a phone has buttons with numbers on

buy give someone money for something

coffee a hot drink

Hi hello

lunchtime the time (usually between 12 o'clock and 2 o'clock) when people stop work to have something to eat

message something you want to tell somebody

party a meeting of friends to eat, drink, talk, dance etc

press push with your finger

ring (*v*) make a sound like a bell (a telephone rings)

sell give someone something, and get money for it

turn off stop something working

voice you speak and sing with your voice

Sally's Phone

ACTIVITIES

Before Reading

1 Look at the front and back cover of the book and choose the correct ending for these sentences.

1 The story happens . . .
a ☐ in the country.
b ☐ in the city.
c ☐ at sea.

2 The story happens . . .
a ☐ in 1950.
b ☐ in 2100.
c ☐ today.

2 Guess what happens.

At the end of the story Sally has got . . .

	Yes	No
1 a new phone.	☐	☐
2 her old phone.	☐	☐
3 a new boyfriend.	☐	☐
4 a new brother.	☐	☐
5 a new car.	☐	☐
6 a new skirt.	☐	☐

While Reading

1 Read pages 1–5. Are these sentences true (T) or false (F)?

1 In the morning, Sally's phone is behind the door.
2 Sally is meeting Jack tonight.
3 Michael is Andrew's boss.
4 Jack does not like Andrew.
5 Lucy is working in High Street.
6 Mary likes Jane's shoes.

2 Read pages 6–9 and answer the questions.

Where . . .
1 . . . is Sally meeting Andrew?
2 . . . does Sally go for a coffee?
Who . . .
3 . . . does not like red?
4 . . . picks up Sally's bag?

3 Read pages 10–13. Who says or thinks these words?

1 'Who's Sally? There's no Sally here.'
2 'What a nice voice!'
3 'It's my birthday.'
4 'Put on your red skirt and go to the party.'

4 Read pages 14–17. Now answer these questions.

1 Why does Paul not know his phone number?

2 Who does Paul phone first?

3 What is the name of Paul's sister?

4 What do Paul and Sally need to do?

5 Where does Sally work?

5 Read pages 18–21. Are these sentences true (T) or false (F)?

1 Louise likes Sally's skirt.

2 Paul has got black hair.

3 Paul is waiting near the trees.

4 They go to Bar Bogart for a drink.

6 Before you read pages 22–24, can you guess what happens?

	Yes	No
1 Paul and Sally meet Andrew.	☑	☑
2 Andrew and Sally go to Bar Bogart.	☑	☑
3 Paul and Sally go to Katharine's party.	☑	☑
4 Andrew phones Sally.	☑	☑
5 Sally phones Andrew.	☑	☑
6 Paul buys flowers for Katharine.	☑	☑
7 Paul buys flowers for Sally.	☑	☑

ACTIVITIES

After Reading

1 Put these sentences in the correct order. Number them 1-10.

a 🗆 Paul finishes his coffee.

b 🗆 Paul says 'I'm sorry,' and he gives the bag to Sally.

c 🗆 She buys a coffee and sits down.

d 🗆 She finishes her coffee and picks up her bag and phone.

e 🗆 Then she goes to the café.

f 🗆 When he stands up, Sally's bag falls on the floor.

g 🗆 Sally goes to the shops with Claire and buys a skirt.

h 🗆 Then he picks up a phone and goes out of the café.

i 🗆 She goes back to work.

j 🗆 She phones her mother and tells her about the new skirt.

2 What do you know about Sally? Write a description using these words.

live/mother/brother
go to work/train
work/friends/Claire and Louise
like/red
has got/boyfriend/Andrew

3 Who says this? Who do they say it to?

1 'Sally, I don't like your hair.'
2 'Bar Bogart. Mmm – that's nice.'
3 'It's beautiful, but I never wear red.'
4 'Red is a good colour for you.'
5 'What's my number?'

4 Complete this summary of the story. Use these words:

Square buys party lunchtime afternoon picks up birthday boyfriend answer coffee

Sally's .... Andrew phones her early in the morning. He wants to meet her that evening. At .... Sally and her friend Claire buy a new skirt for Sally. Then Sally has a .... in a café. When Sally's bag falls to the floor, Sally meets Paul. He .... her bag, but he takes her phone – and Sally takes his phone. That .... , Andrew phones Sally – but he talks to Paul. Paul's sister wants to tell him about her .... party – but she speaks to Sally. In the end, Paul phones Sally, and they meet after work in Queen's .... Paul .... some flowers for his sister, and he and Sally go to her .... Andrew phones Sally, but she does not ....

ABOUT THE AUTHOR

Christine Lindop was born in New Zealand and taught English in France and Spain before moving to Britain. She has written many books, including several for the Oxford Bookworms Library. These include *Ned Kelly* (Stage 1) and *Australia and New Zealand* (Stage 3). She has also written for other Oxford readers series, including Dominoes and Classic Tales.

OXFORD BOOKWORMS LIBRARY

Classics • Crime & Mystery • Factfiles • Fantasy & Horror
Human Interest • Playscripts • Thriller & Adventure
True Stories • World Stories

The OXFORD BOOKWORMS LIBRARY provides enjoyable reading in English, with a wide range of classic and modern fiction, non-fiction, and plays. It includes original and adapted texts in seven carefully graded language stages, which take learners from beginner to advanced level. An overview is given on the next pages.

All Stage 1 titles are available as audio recordings, as well as over eighty other titles from Starter to Stage 6. All Starters and many titles at Stages 1 to 4 are specially recommended for younger learners. Every Bookworm is illustrated, and Starters and Factfiles have full-colour illustrations.

The OXFORD BOOKWORMS LIBRARY also offers extensive support. Each book contains an introduction to the story, notes about the author, a glossary, and activities. Additional resources include tests and worksheets, and answers for these and for the activities in the books. There is advice on running a class library, using audio recordings, and the many ways of using Oxford Bookworms in reading programmes. Resource materials are available on the website <www.oup.com/bookworms>.

The *Oxford Bookworms Collection* is a series for advanced learners. It consists of volumes of short stories by well-known authors, both classic and modern. Texts are not abridged or adapted in any way, but carefully selected to be accessible to the advanced student.

You can find details and a full list of titles in the *Oxford Bookworms Library Catalogue* and *Oxford English Language Teaching Catalogues*, and on the website <www.oup.com/bookworms>.

THE OXFORD BOOKWORMS LIBRARY
GRADING AND SAMPLE EXTRACTS

STARTER • 250 HEADWORDS

present simple – present continuous – imperative –
can/cannot, must – *going to* (future) – simple gerunds ...

Her phone is ringing – but where is it?

Sally gets out of bed and looks in her bag. No phone.
She looks under the bed. No phone. Then she looks
behind the door. There is her phone. Sally picks up her
phone and answers it. *Sally's Phone*

STAGE 1 ●400◉ HEADWORDS

... past simple – coordination with *and, but, or* –
subordination with *before, after, when, because, so* ...

I knew him in Persia. He was a famous builder and I
worked with him there. For a time I was his friend, but
not for long. When he came to Paris, I came after him –
I wanted to watch him. He was a very clever, very
dangerous man. *The Phantom of the Opera*

STAGE 2 • 700 HEADWORDS

... present perfect – *will* (future) – *(don't) have to, must not, could* –
comparison of adjectives – simple *if* clauses – past continuous –
tag questions – *ask/tell* + infinitive ...

While I was writing these words in my diary, I decided
what to do. I must try to escape. I shall try to get down
the wall outside. The window is high above the ground,
but I have to try. I shall take some of the gold with me –
if I escape, perhaps it will be helpful later. *Dracula*

STAGE 3 • 1000 HEADWORDS

... should, may – present perfect continuous – *used to* – past perfect –
causative – relative clauses – indirect statements ...

Of course, it was most important that no one should see
Colin, Mary, or Dickon entering the secret garden. So Colin
gave orders to the gardeners that they must all keep away
from that part of the garden in future. *The Secret Garden*

STAGE 4 • 1400 HEADWORDS

... past perfect continuous – passive (simple forms) –
would conditional clauses – indirect questions –
relatives with *where/when* – gerunds after prepositions/phrases ...

I was glad. Now Hyde could not show his face to the world
again. If he did, every honest man in London would be
proud to report him to the police. *Dr Jekyll and Mr Hyde*

STAGE 5 • 1800 HEADWORDS

... future continuous – future perfect –
passive (modals, continuous forms) –
would have conditional clauses – modals + perfect infinitive ...

If he had spoken Estella's name, I would have hit him. I was so
angry with him, and so depressed about my future, that I could
not eat the breakfast. Instead I went straight to the old house.
Great Expectations

STAGE 6 • 2500 HEADWORDS

... passive (infinitives, gerunds) – advanced modal meanings –
clauses of concession, condition

When I stepped up to the piano, I was confident. It was as if I
knew that the prodigy side of me really did exist. And when I
started to play, I was so caught up in how lovely I looked that
I didn't worry how I would sound. *The Joy Luck Club*

Star Reporter

JOHN ESCOTT

'There's a new girl in town,' says Joe, and soon Steve is out looking for her. Marietta is easy to find in a small town, but every time he sees her something goes wrong . . . and his day goes from bad to worse.

Survive!

HELEN BROOKE

You are in a small plane, going across the Rocky Mountains. Suddenly, the engine starts to make strange noises . . .

Soon you are alone, in the snow, at the top of a mountain, and it is very, very cold. Can you find your way out of the mountain?

Orca

PHILLIP BURROWS AND MARK FOSTER

When Tonya and her friends decide to sail around the world they want to see exciting things and visit exciting places.

But one day, they meet an orca – a killer whale – one of the most dangerous animals in the sea. And life gets a little too exciting.

The Fifteenth Character

ROSEMARY BORDER

'It's an interesting job,' says Sally about her work at Happy Hills. And today is a very exciting day because Zapp the famous singer is coming. Everybody is having a wonderful time. But suddenly something goes wrong – very wrong.

BOOKWORMS · HUMAN INTEREST · STAGE 1

Christmas in Prague

JOYCE HANNAM

In a house in Oxford three people are having breakfast – Carol, her husband Jan, and his father Josef. They are talking about Prague, because Carol wants them all to go there for Christmas.

Josef was born in Prague, but he left his home city when he was a young man. He is an old man now, and he would like to see Prague again before he dies. But he is afraid. He still remembers another Christmas in Prague, many long years ago – a Christmas that changed his life for ever . . .

BOOKWORMS · TRUE STORIES · STAGE 1

Ned Kelly: A True Story

CHRISTINE LINDOP

When he was a boy, he was poor and hungry. When he was a young man, he was still poor and still hungry. He learnt how to steal horses, he learnt how to fight, he learnt how to live – outside the law. Australia in the 1870s was a hard, wild place. Rich people had land, poor people didn't. So the rich got richer, and the poor stayed poor.

Some say Ned Kelly was a bad man. Some say he was a good man but the law was bad. This is the true story of Australia's most famous outlaw.